LIFE BY THE

RIVER

By Holly Duhig

BookLife
PUBLISHING

©2019
BookLife Publishing Ltd.
King's Lynn
Norfolk PE30 4LS

ISBN: 978-1-78637-585-8

Written by:
Holly Duhig

Edited by:
Emilie Dufresne

Designed by:
Amy Li

All rights reserved.
Printed in Malaysia.

CONTENTS

Words that look like **this** can be found in the glossary on page 24.

HUMAN HABITATS

POLAR BEAR

A habitat is a place that provides a living thing with food, water and shelter. An animal's body needs to be adapted to its habitat. For example, polar bears need thick fur so they can survive in their Arctic habitat.

Humans also have habitats. Unlike most animals, humans can survive in many different habitats and our bodies don't need to be adapted to them. Some human habitats are pretty extreme!

Humans don't have thick fur but we can make fur coats.

RIVER HABITATS

HOUSEBOATS IN INDIA

People all over the world live on rivers and lakes. They provide people with food, water and a way of getting around. Rivers can be a human habitat.

People have lived by rivers for thousands of years because they are very useful for trading things by boat or ship. Cities such as London, Paris and Rome were all built around rivers.

TIBER RIVER IN ROME

LIFE BY THE GANGES

The Ganges is considered **sacred** to followers of Hinduism.

Rivers are important for food, water and trade, but are also important for other reasons. For example, the Ganges, a river in India, plays an important role in people's religion.

Millions of Hindus visit the Ganges to bathe in its waters. It is believed the water is sacred and bathing in it can cure people of illnesses. It is also believed that the water can cleanse them of their sins.

Hindus collect water from the Ganges to take back to sick family members.

USING THE RIVER

The city of Varanasi was built around the banks of the Ganges. Some people in the city use the river water for washing, cooking and bathing. The river is very useful for people who live in this city.

The Ganges is important at all stages of people's lives, even after they die. Bodies are cremated at the Ganges because it is thought that the river will carry them to the afterlife.

LIFE BY THE TONLÉ SAP

Half of the fish eaten in Cambodia come from the Tonlé Sap.

The Tonlé Sap is a large lake connected to the Tonlé Sap River in Cambodia which supports many floating villages. The Tonlé Sap Lake is home to over 300 species of fish.

During the rainy season, from June to October, the lake fills with water and grows to 10,000 square kilometres. In the dry season, from November to May, it shrinks in size to 3,000 square kilometres.

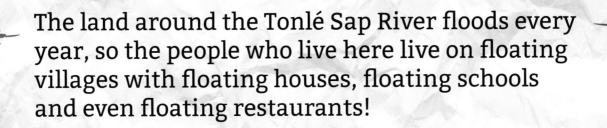

The land around the Tonlé Sap River floods every year, so the people who live here live on floating villages with floating houses, floating schools and even floating restaurants!

There are also houses built on stilts around the lake.

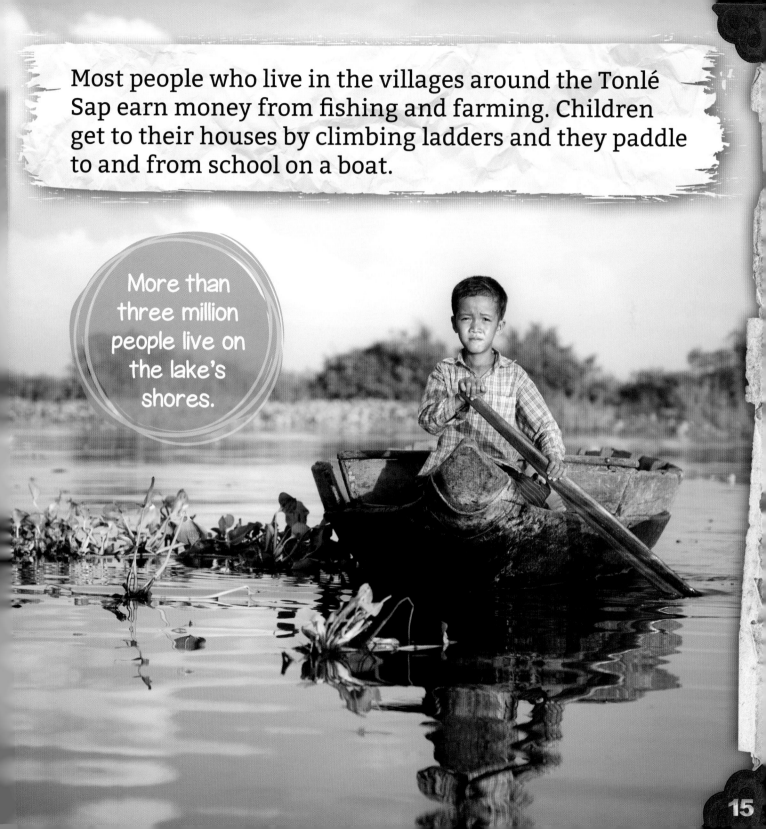

Most people who live in the villages around the Tonlé Sap earn money from fishing and farming. Children get to their houses by climbing ladders and they paddle to and from school on a boat.

More than three million people live on the lake's shores.

LIFE ON LAKE TITICACA

Lake Titicaca is one of the largest lakes in South America.

On Lake Titicaca, between Peru and Bolivia, there are people who live on floating islands made out of reeds. The islands were made by the Uros people so they could protect themselves.

Life on the floating islands is quite traditional but the Uros people have lots of modern technology too. Their boats have motors and they have televisions and their own radio station too.

MAKING THE ISLANDS

The Uros people make the islands by weaving layers and layers of dried reeds that grow in the lake. The reeds can also be used for food and as building materials.

The Uros people use flowers from the reeds to make tea.

The islands are held in place using sticks and ropes.

Lake Titicaca provides the Uros people with fish which are an important source of food. Many of the islands are made with holes in the middle of them for fishing.

LIFE ON A
HOUSEBOAT

Over 15,000 people in the UK live on waterways.

A houseboat is a boat that people live in. People all over the world live in houseboats. Boats made for England's narrow canals can't be more than 2 metres wide!

LOCKS

LOCK

Water doesn't flow uphill, so waterways use locks to allow boats to raise and lower the boats across different levels.

Locks are **chambers** with gates on each end. Each chamber holds water, and the water can be raised or lowered to match the level at the next lock, raising or lowering the boat with it.

There are over 1,500 locks in England and Wales.

ACTIVITY

Can you think of five words that describe where you live?

IS THE WEATHER COLD WHERE YOU LIVE?

OR IS THE WEATHER HOT WHERE YOU LIVE?

People have many ways of adapting to their own human habitat. Perhaps you live in a cold country and have to wrap up warm. Or maybe you live in a hot country and have to wear a sunhat?

GLOSSARY

ADAPTED	changed over time to suit the environment
AFTERLIFE	a religious belief that there is another life after death
CHAMBERS	enclosed spaces or cavities
CREMATED	to have burnt a dead body to ashes
SACRED	connected to a god or gods
SINS	acts that are considered bad or wrong by religions
SPECIES	a group of very similar animals or plants that are capable of producing young together
SQUARE KILOMETRES	a measurement of an area that is a square with each side being a kilometre in length
TRADING	buying and selling goods
TRADITIONAL	related to very old behaviours or beliefs
WEAVING	criss-crossing long threads or reeds to make a usable material

INDEX

Please renew or return items by the date shown on your receipt

www.hertfordshire.gov.uk/libraries

Renewals and enquiries: 0300 123 4049

Textphone for hearing or 0300 123 4041
speech impaired users:

L32 11.16

528 747 67 9

SoT

Please renew or return items by the date shown on your receipt

www.hertfordshire.gov.uk/libraries

Renewals and enquiries: 0300 123 4049

Textphone for hearing or 0300 123 4041
speech impaired users:

L32 11.16

Hertfordshire

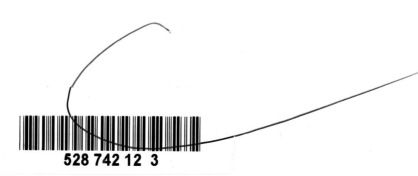

528 742 12 3